AN INTENSE CALM
Maldives Eco Surfing Chronicle

By ThiruMoolar Devar

www.EarthAfloatPublishing.com

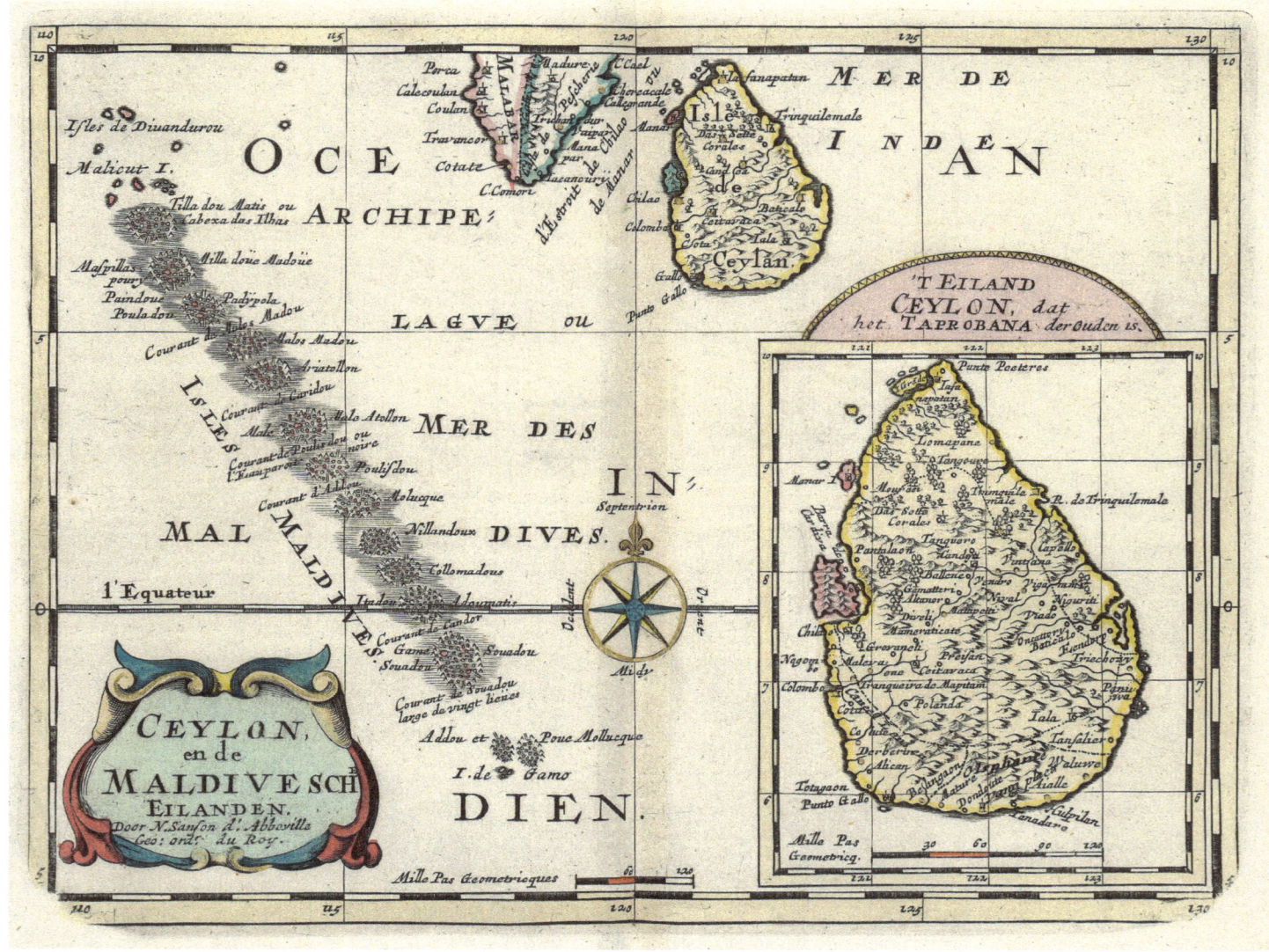

Nicolas Sanson 1600 - 1677 / Public domain

An Intense Calm - Maldives Eco Surfing Chronicles
Copyright © 2020 by ThiruMoolar Devar
All rights reserved. No part of this book may be reproduced or used in any manner without written permission of the copyright owner except for the use of quotations in a book review.
ISBN: 978-1-7353953-5-7 (Paperback)
ISBN: 978-1-7353953-3-3 (Kindle)
ISBN: 978-1-7353953-7-1 (ePub)

Table of Contents

Preface: Indian Ocean Quarantine Diary 5

Prologue: Epiphany. 9

  I   Breathe. 13

  II   Timing, Rhythm, Waves, & Cycles 19

  III   Launch 27

  IV   No Limits vs. Know Your limits 35

  V   Look All Ways. 41

  VI   Return. 47

  VII   Local Knowledge 53

  VIII   In The Vortex 67

  IX   Euphoria. 75

  X   The Meaning of Life 83

Epilogue: Ego. 93

Author's Bio. 99

Fables Found 100

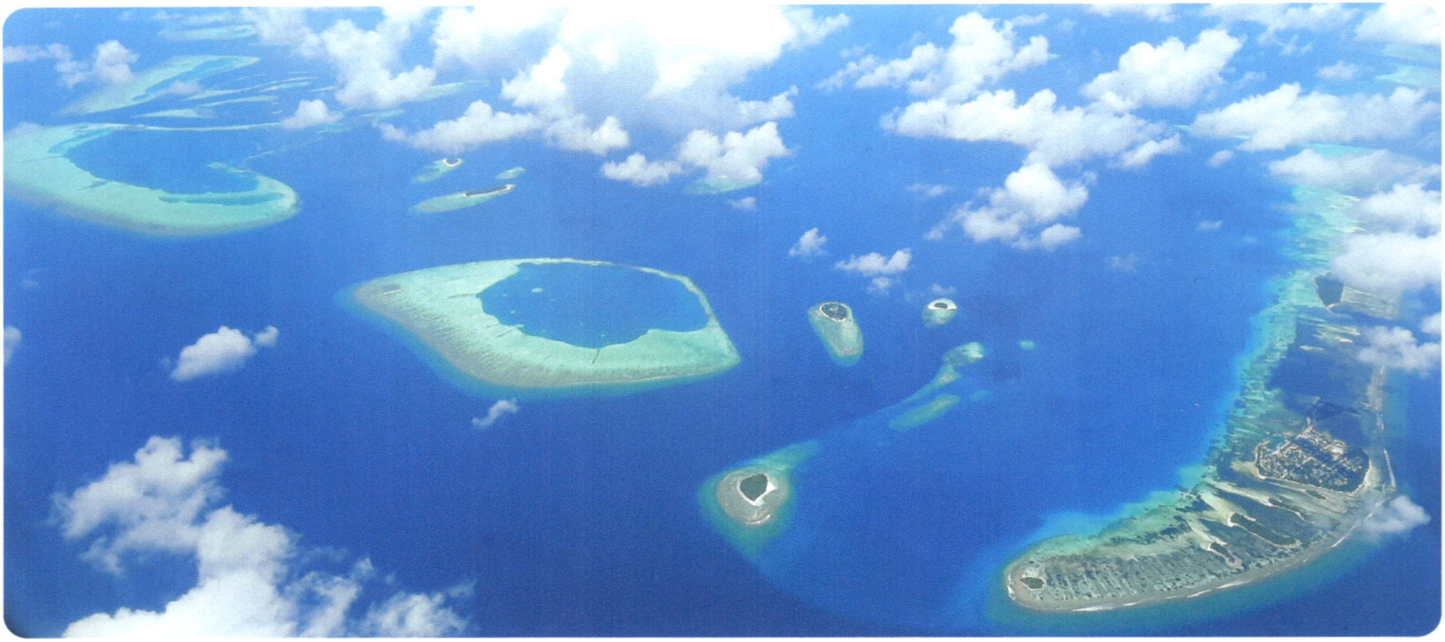

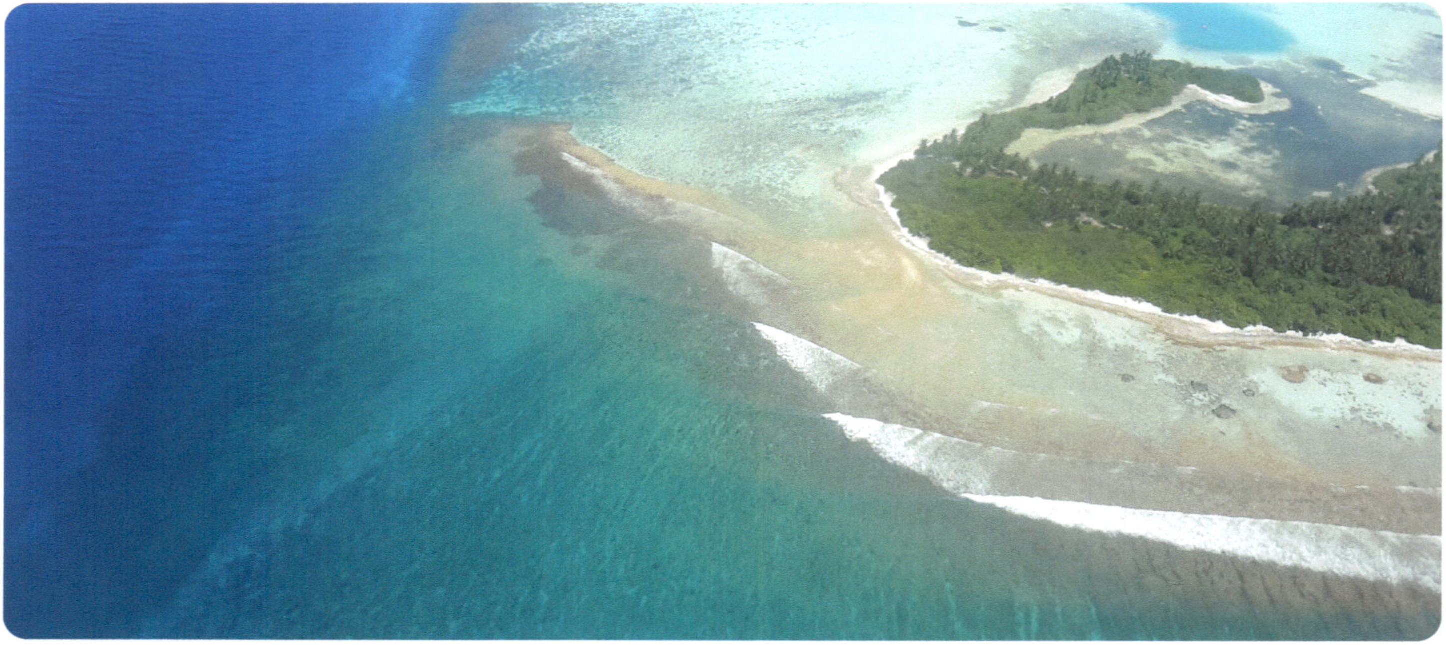

Preface

Indian Ocean Quarantine Diary

Well, I've arrived at the wrong place right at the wrong time before. In 2020 however, it seems that my arrival in the Maldives was at least the "right place at the wrong time." And, it seems it was a year plus in the making.

I spent the entire 2019 on a clockwise trip around the world, to decide where I wanted to spend the next 50 years, as I was to turn 50 in July 2020 (Now, past tense, as I write this). By January 2020, I had decided to base out of Cambodia as a central spot to launch surf and explore missions to the Maldives, Indonesia, and the West Pacific.

In February, I set up my apartment and office in Siem Reap, Cambodia. In early March, I paid a couple of months' rent in advance and hopped over to the Maldives for some exploration and surf to seal my new plan as a success. However, the world had a different strategy for me. Countries closed borders, airlines canceled flights, and COVID-19 Lockdowns put into effect.

And that brings us to today. It's late August, almost half a year later. I'm on a small island in the Indian Ocean, waiting to see if I'll find a flight back to my apartment in Cambodia before I lose it. I paid rent for five months I wasn't there, and now my deposit has been applied to a final extra month before my multi-entry VISA expires. Soon, I'll find out what the future has planned next.

**Update: August 30, 2020 - I lost my apartment, the property manager double-rented it, quit & split with the $$. My stuff is so far unaccounted for and may be lost to the wind... hmm.. what should I do next? I guess I'm still a nomad...

Dedicated to the Maldivian wave riders.

**Note to self: You can make plans, but the world doesn't always adhere to them.

Prologue: Epiphany

In my quest for meaning, for the marking of time, and to generally make good use of time, I sought out an epiphany during my Maldives island sojourn. The act of searching is, in itself, a way of life. Never stop learning. Exercise of the mind's curiosity is a map to the fabled fountain of youth.

Journal Entry:

My last epiphany took place just over 20 years ago. I was 29 years old. As I was awakening from sleep on that day, my mind played a trick on me. I thought I was 80 years old. As I lay in bed, with my eyes closed, reflecting on my life, I felt a little disappointed. I thought, "wow. There were so many ideas, plans, and dreams I had for my life that I didn't even try to achieve. And now, it's too late."

Within maybe fractions of a second, I realized my disorientation, and that in half a year, I'd be turning 30 years old. There was a feeling as if I'd won the lottery or a Sweepstakes. The "gift" of now having 50 years in front of me, before once again, I may wake up in the morning and reflect upon my life, was tremendously elating.

Hence, a fire was lit under my rear to get a move on it and, at the very least, attempt the things I know are possible. That, to fail, will not be the thing that disappoints me on my last days. It would be that I didn't try.

Last year, I visited the Maldives for the first time. That was a goal and a dream come true that I'd decided upon exactly one-year prior. Indeed, it was the initial decision to go to the Maldives that itself expanded into my 2019 one-year clockwise trip around the world. The discoveries made on that trip are why consciously or unconsciously, I "chose" to get locked-down in the Maldives.

To put everything on the line, as I've done more than once, suggests I'd have to be reasonably confident of my ability to rebuild from scratch. And, I can take solace in that.

*If you don't start it, will never happen
the year and decade passes fast
forge ahead; embarkment is the hard part
when the adventure is underway,
the doubts will fade away*

Chasing Immortality to the Last Breath

Breathe

Life in the Maldives is one of integration with nature and a feeling of awe for these enchanting isles that invoke a sense of "heaven on Earth."

The South Asia country has an elevation of just 1.5m, making it the lowest in the world. The archipelago stretches across 90,000 square kilometers. There are about 1200 islands in a chain of 26 atolls. From top to bottom, it's 820 km from northern-most island to Addu atoll south of the equator. It's 130 km from east to west. Most of the islands are uninhabited, and some are not much more than slabs of coral and a pile of sand with a palm tree or two.

Journal Entry:

Relinquishing the sentimental articles of my past was a process that took years. I am an escapee of the "consumption" lifestyle.

In our minds, there is an opportunity to practice minimalism too. As with the external world, we tend to compartmentalize to sort and organize thoughts just as with possessions.

But how can one consider the universe to be minimal with all its variety and moods? Being tethered to unnecessary belongings can be an obstacle to a dynamic relationship with our Mother Earth.

The further one gets from the extraneous "things" we think we need, the closer we can integrate with our environment. While material goods can bring great satisfaction, we shouldn't lose sight of the authentic joys realized in the amazingly sophisticated, yet simplicity of the planet.

The more we're aware of our environment, the slower time goes by, allowing us to assimilate the world's moments with heightened intuition. Whether or not we are conscious of the subtle details, they still exist, regardless of our recognition or acknowledgment.

Therefore, minimalism is a process by which we can squeeze the essence out of life's juiciest moments, thereby achieving the maximum!!

We are a part of nature, not separate from it.

The search for the perfect wave is akin to the age-old quest to learn the meaning of life.

If "time is of the essence," then, not to say whether fast or slow; but to promote good timing either with haste or hesitation...

Timing, Rhythm, Waves, & Cycles

The equatorial weather and elements in the Maldives are relatively mild-mannered compared to other latitudes. However, like anywhere else, it serves one well to be aware of the surroundings and environment.

There are only two main seasons. Iruvai, the north-east monsoon, translated from the local Dhivehi language means, "hot and dry." It runs from mid-January to mid-April. Hulhangu is the south-west monsoon, meaning, "hot and west," and generally runs the other half of the year, from mid-April through to mid-December.

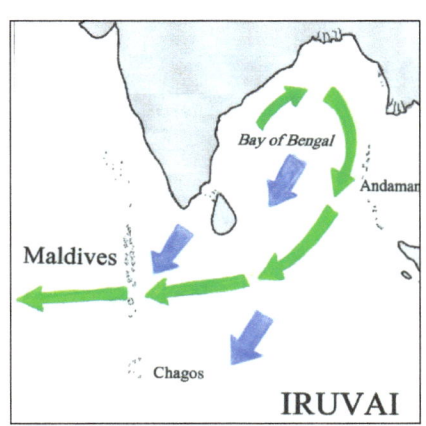

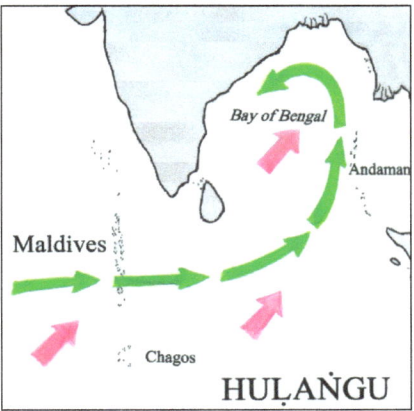

https://commons.wikimedia.org/wiki/File:Maldives_seasons3.jpg
Xavier Romero-Frias / CC BY (https://creativecommons.org/licenses/by/3.0)

Journal Entry:

Life is a game of odds.

If opening a door requires a combination, how long might it take to discover it?

If it takes a long time to open the door, don't get discouraged because when the portal does open, it's the game-changer you were seeking.

In life, we know that to succeed, it's essential to understand the price of failure. The pursuit of perfection is a process of trial and error.

A bird must build a new nest in response to environmental demands.

So too, we should be prepared to start anew, however many times is required to first, sustain our existence and survive, and second, to thrive.

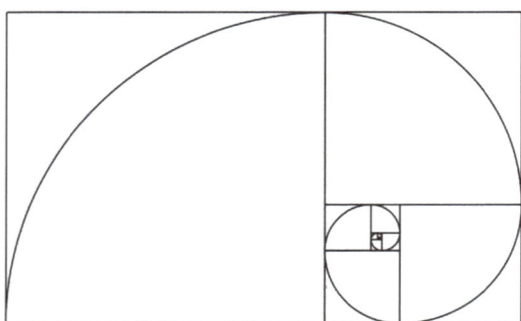

Rider: Bro

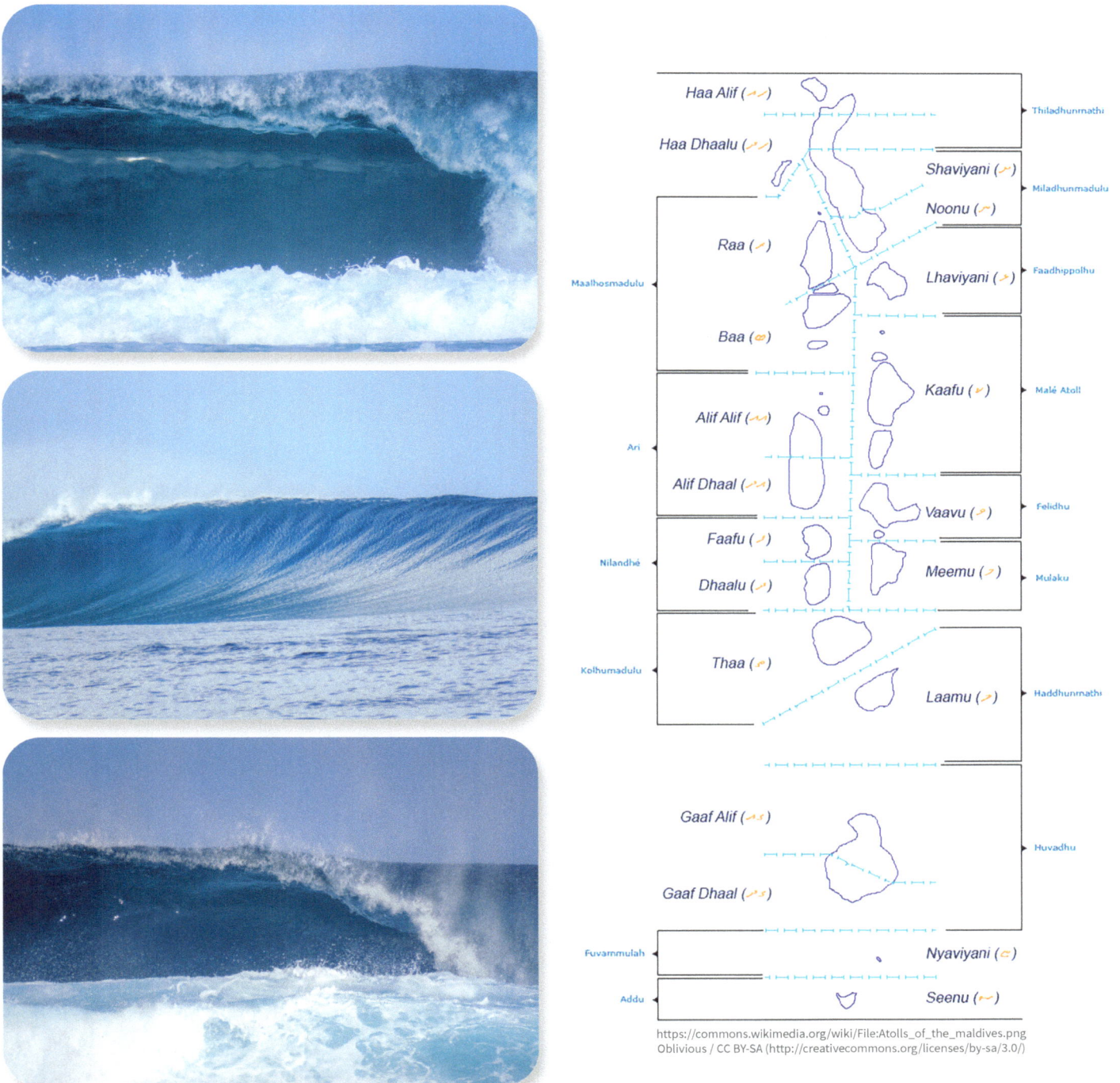

Rider Fayani

Launch

The Maldives was an important crossroads in the ancient spice route. Seafarers traversing the Indian Ocean stopped for supplies or due to shipwrecks sailing between Asia, Africa, and the Arab world. The country's culture and traditions revolve around the sea, and of course, fishing, the always abundant food source.

The stylish Dhoni is unique to the Maldives and their direct neighbors Sri Lanka and South India. The earliest boats had sails, commonly built from the wood of coconut trees. Nowadays, motors have replaced most sails.

Journal Entry:

Make life deliberate. Balance and temperament are crucial for an accurate perception of our ever-changing environment. Let not the state of being relaxed be expressed in laziness. Do not construe alertness to nail-biting anxiety. Be still, yet ready to go from zero to max velocity in split seconds. Maintain tenacious confidence to accelerate with a guided precision.

Preparing for the worst scenarios seems a bit like Murphy's Law. If I have a first aid kit, I may never need it. The other side of the coin is to need it and not have it. A better option is to pay ahead for preparedness and potential prevention than have a surprise calamity.

For centuries humans strive to command the sea yet are quickly lost in our original deep space frontier. Stretch limbs, eat smart, drink water, and check the equipment. After leaving the land, we will be at the mercy of creatures and elements far beyond our natural realm and comfort zone.

Inner calm is the most practical survival skill. Our first necessity for life is oxygen. Panic causes the body to lose oxygen rapidly. Fear may be reasonable at times to encourage caution. Panicking is never beneficial to any situation, ever.

Finally, it serves us wisely always to speak well, as we won't know when that communication might be our famous last words.

Form without function is like a car with no engine; its usefulness won't go far.

The Art of being at peace in the middle of a storm

Poised in serenity and awareness
perseverance through the pain
yet more so, the fear of pain

Calm, positive aspiration

This physical body is
a tiny yet quite substantial
part of the experience.

I realize the intensity of
the situation at hand and
it lends to an occasional
tendency to pre-react…

No Limits vs. Know Your Limits

Can people fly? Well, that's debatable, but numerous have perished reinventing wings. Taking a lesson from the legend of Icarus, beware of surfing too close to the sun. The sun's rays are particularly strong on the equator shining at a direct 90° angle

Don't underestimate the sun while in the refreshing ocean. Water tends to magnify the sun's strength. Hydration and plenty of drinking water is crucial to prevent heatstroke. Sunscreens will to wear off faster than usual.

*Be sure to travel prepared with reef-safe sunscreen that uses approved ingredients not containing coral damaging chemicals.

**Watch out for falling coconuts. Be aware of where you stand!

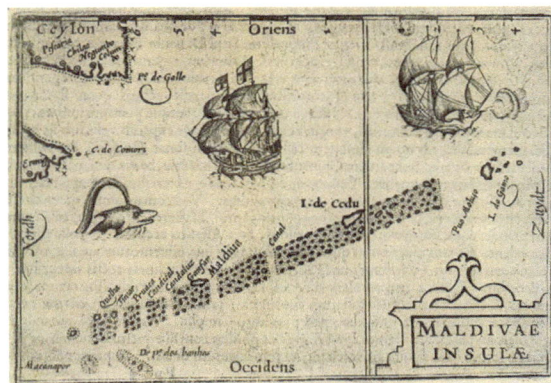

Bertius / Public domain https://commons.wikimedia.org/wiki/File:1598_Middleburg_Bertius_Maldives_map_latin.jpg

Journal Entry:

Once upon a time, a man looked at a bird and said, "I want to fly." I wonder how many folks have called other people dumb for incessantly jumping off buildings with homemade wings? How many so-called inventors died? Nevertheless, no one questions the reality of humans flying anymore; it's standard practice.

The Foremost enemy in our lives is ourselves. In sports, one reason injuries can happen in unassuming, and comfortable conditions are the nonchalant approach to the elements when we're not so intimidated. Likewise, one reason pushing your limits surfing on a challenging swell improves your ability, is because you're then less afraid of less demanding waves. Hence, pushing the boundaries, balanced with respect for even the most docile of environments, will keep us safely performing at our highest levels.

As they say, "Choose Your Battles." Gravity is a general challenge and a particular enemy to our bodies as we age. From childhood into youth and adulthood, we push upwards in maybe the most natural opposition to the earth's gravitational pull on our bodies. Somewhere in the 30s and 40s, we hit a physical plateau and upward zenith point. After that, if we've made it thus far in good health, we're probably learning that to retain some youthful aspects to our existence, we'll have to narrow in on the crucial battle with the planet's magnetic field.

Rider: Leo

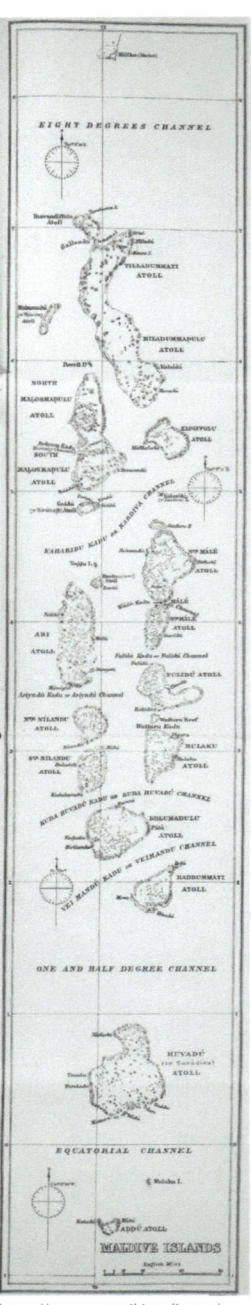

https://commons.wikimedia.org/wiki/File:British_Colonial_era_map_of_Maldives.gif Unknown author / CC BY-SA (https://creativecommons.org/licenses/by-sa/3.0)

Gravity is our playmate

Rider: Sippe'

Where is the point of no return?
I don't know, but
at that point
I've arrived and
still have not quite
gotten the point...
therein lies my continued
drive for adventure
and no return!

*wow.. great form.. i'm not kidding,
i wish i had such stylish wipeouts...*

Look All Ways

Every year wave riders and beach enthusiasts travel to the Maldives from around the world. It is rightly known as one of the best ocean sport wonderlands, and most desirable places to go. A nice thing about arriving in the Maldives is that it's convenient and hassle-free. You'll step off your plane, pass through customs, and step directly onto a speedboat that takes you to your hotel or charter boat.

Before 2008, tourists went only to the high-end exclusive resorts and did not visit the resident islands. Today's tourism industry has diversified. The general population has opened guest lodges and tour operations that accommodate varying budgets.

Observe the signs.

Journal Entry:

When we learn to walk, we're taught to look both ways crossing the street. How can someone know what's going on if they're only looking one way?

Don't take anything for granted.

Learning a new spot is an awesome experience. At first, there are many unknowns regarding the ocean floor, the current, where to sit, and how to escape.

Check out the scene, take your time. Watch the ocean and study the waves from close and from afar. When embarking, grip the rocks, careful not to step on a loose stone, causing a damaging fall to body and board. For valuable lessons, observe the crab, a master of scurrying across slippery rocks.

Getting to know the subtleties and nuances of a new surf spot has great rewards. Build a relationship with the barnacles, boulders, reefs, currents, tides, and wind.

Besides being a strong swimmer, there is no equivalent boost to self-confidence than having a solid plan b. It's crucial to know alternate routes for return to land under varying conditions and circumstances.

There is a multitude of hidden clues to discover when learning a new spot. The affair is increasingly enthralling as the mystery becomes a familiar mental map of a terrain unseen.

Crossing a one-way street still requires looking both ways.

*Regular foot,
it's all good
Goofy foot,
in the hood*

*Flipper foot
return to land
to plant your feet
in the sand*

Return

Stepping away from the hustle and bustle of the city island of Malé or the luxurious high-end resorts, one immediately feels the sensation of going back in time.

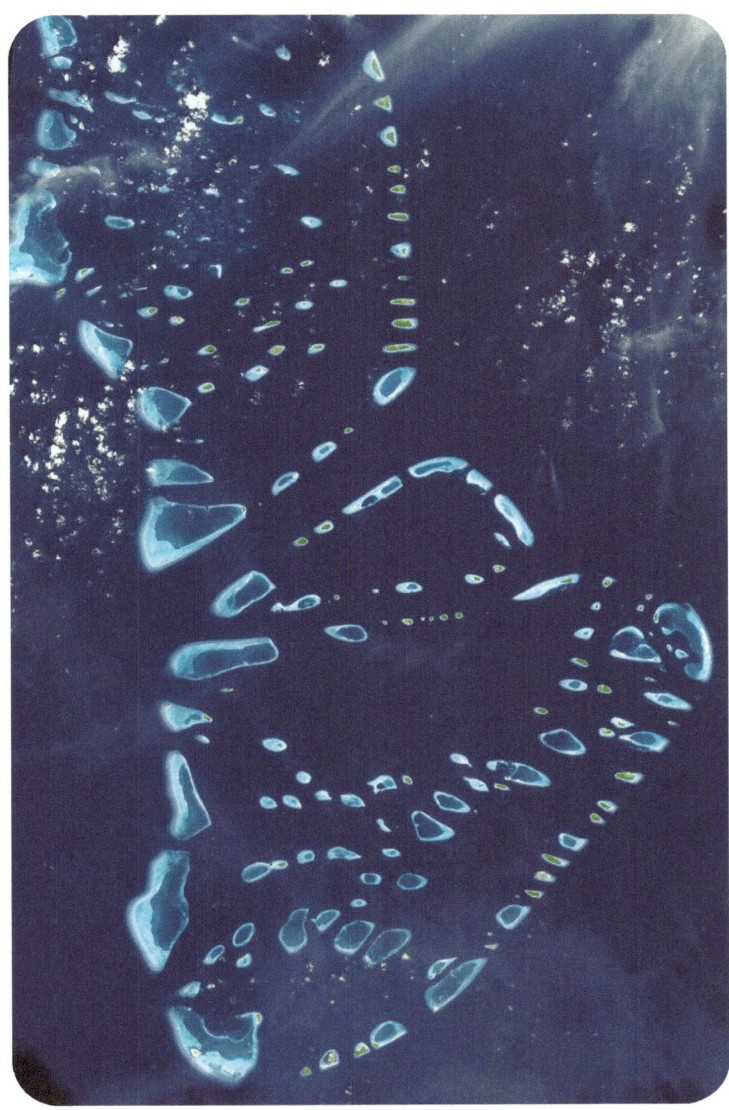

https://www.goodfreephotos.com/public-domain-images/satellite-image-of-the-maldives.jpg.php

There is a sense of pristine cleanliness in this island chain of pearls. It becomes evident that people have a heightened sense of tidiness and organization seen in the daily activity of routine and maintenance.

Simultaneously, the Maldives has all the modern amenities, cell towers, internet, and in fact, among the highest literacy rates internationally. A return to basics coexists with reaching for the stars.

Journal Entry:

Where shall i take nomadic refuge?

I recall times that I had nowhere particular to go. I would pull my truck off to the side of the road and sit there, pondering my destination instead of driving around aimlessly.

In this digital age time flies in front of screens. It seems periods pass while living more in the mind than the body. Returning to the physical realm involves attentiveness to the body's needs, such as water, nutritious food, and solid sleep. You get out what you put in.

As technology has made survival more automated, our antennae radar-like instincts (often referred to as "intuition") are less required. As the expression says, "if you don't use it, you lose it." Is there an opposite of evolution? By definition, no.

The best surfers have an unspoken sort of psychic intuition of the waves to predict their behavior.

Total immersion is required. Allow time to slow down. Did you ever watch a patient predator perched in wait for the right moment to strike?

*The moon has got me on a leash
and tugs at me now and then*

the sun soothes my soul

*my nocturnal insomnia is such that
i watched the moonrise at sunset and
i watched the moonset at sunrise... zzzzzz*

Local Knowledge

Due to a small population and a unique, tight-knit community, the Maldivian people have a mellow vibe with less pressure than most societies in the world. They are very friendly. In some places, they have rarely seen foreigners, so it can help to break the ice by taking the initiative to say hello!

The spoken and written language of the Maldives is Dhivehi. At the time of this writing and not expected anytime soon, Dhivehi is not in Google Translate. It's a hybrid comprised of the peoples who've influenced the archipelago, including English, Hindustani, Portuguese, Persian, French, and Arabic. The writing and characters of the alphabet have an Arabic influence.

Stories have lain hidden for centuries scattered across the atolls. One could spend a lifetime exploring its corners, learning about the previous generations, and history of ancient explorers in these remote and hard to reach parts of Earth.

Journal Entry:

You'll never see a place from the eyes of someone with the consciousness of generations.

For every generation, there is a preceding generation that paved the way to this point. Work hard to contribute to the future. Without the contributions of our ancestors, we would not have arrived by way of an already carved path today.

The route to knowing the real secrets is to glean local knowledge. Consider yourself lucky to be in the graces of those who will impart a glimpse of the essence and vibrations of a foreign country's culture.

When in the water or on the land, please consider the children, the beginners, and the elderly. Show regard for those at the top of the food chain too, whether leaders, followers or independents.

Remember, that waves are like gold. We are no longer in the times of embarking on missions to distant shores to take resources from the innocent and often people that don't have the opportunity to jet-set as you do.

Rider: Farey

If you arrive at the line-up for the first time and paddle past locals to a priority position, it is a sign of disrespect. Sometimes this is excused by the fair assumption the visitor has low social intelligence and culture. It doesn't matter how good you look "stealing treasures," it won't earn you the respect of the locals

Indeed, many surfers travel far for quick visits and spend a lot of money in a short period. A common tendency is to feel pressure and even an entitlement to getting a wave quota per dollar, so to speak. But that's a mistake that can lower the actual value of an adventure. Focus on the moment and not the outcome.

Don't have an entitled attitude because you're a tourist and supposedly financing the residents. While your cash may be appreciated, bad behavior will not earn respect.

Surfers are part of a great international club. The wise empath will adhere to the standard rules and etiquette, which does not take a genius to understand.

Rider Ammaday

Rider Shimoo

Rider Hupa

Rider Hishaam

Rider Adam

Rider Shimatey

Rider Aya

Rider Dhoonii

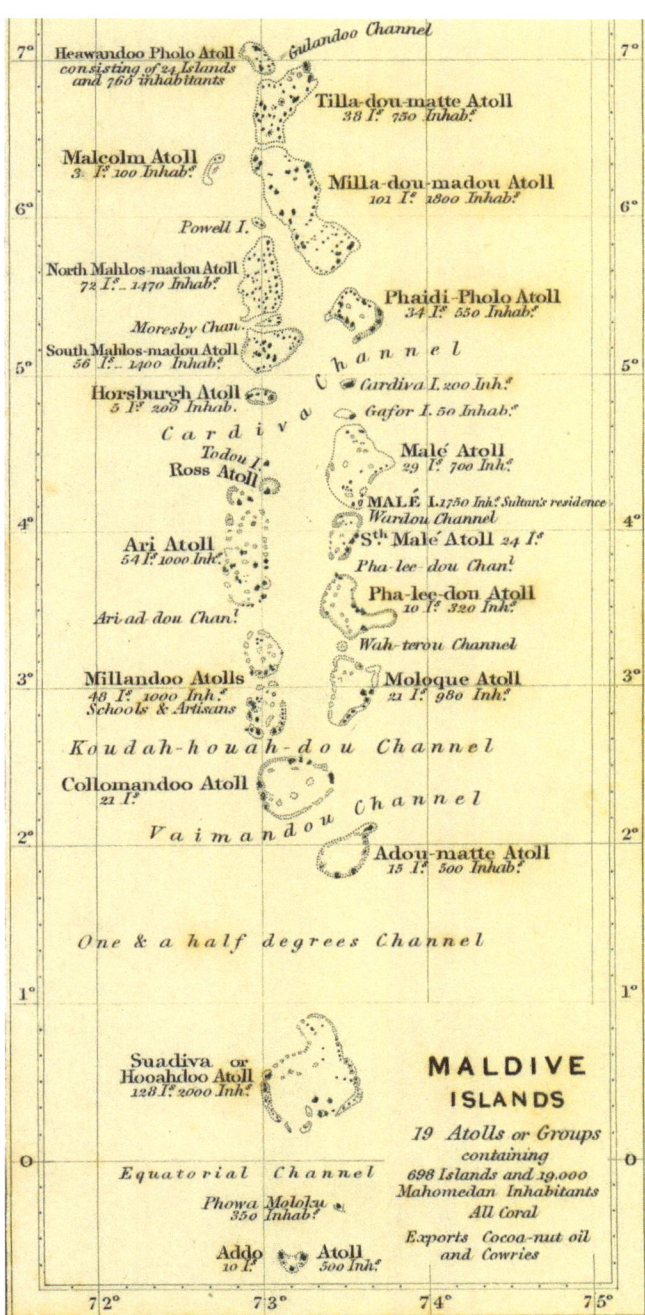

I. J. and C. Walker, Society for the Diffusion of Useful Knowledge (Great Britain), Chapman and Hall / Public domain 1844

Mystery Rider

In The Vortex

Tube riding the spinning vortex of organized chaos is the pinnacle of the surfing experience. Barrels abound to make the Maldives a magical mecca and wave-filled wonderland.

Time slows down for those who can harness peace and awareness in a fast and fluid blue womb of saltwater.

Journal Entry:

Belief is perhaps the most potent of human traits. Many draw a bold dividing line and accept concepts only when pre-approved by the science establishment. That's a counter-intuitive approach to our unique creative abilities. Placebos are a scientific phenomenon. It's proven, pills can cure headaches with no particular medicine besides the claim that it heals. A belief that eliminates physical pain and also gives us confident faith to survive and thrive is an asset to life. If a person positively harnesses the potential of belief, it can be a powerful vehicle for the realization of miracles.

It may be tough to pinpoint what exactly is reality, especially juxtaposed, with all of the varying perceptions and points of view. For sure, what one believes will largely shape their truth and actuality. Hence, I suggest, given a choice -choose your beliefs wisely!

When you're doing what you want to be doing, and you know it's what you want to be doing forever

Mystery Rider

If you have experienced this fusion to end all confusion then you have witnessed miracles.

Rider Ajey

Suffice it to say; it would take a miracle to transcend the chaos of the universe to perceive eternal order.

Rider: Kuda Ayya

Rider Anko

Peaceful vibrations
and vibrant colors are
bound to put your

mind and body
to tranquil ease.

Euphoria

The species and habitats of the Maldives exemplify astonishing and beautiful biodiversity. Mangroves create an entire ecosystem, and like other wetlands around the world, they are facing a high risk of erasure by development. The diverse companion ecosystem, rightfully known as "rainforests of the sea," is the shallow coral reefs.

Indeed, the majority of the Maldives is of water; hence, the majority of animal life is aquatic. From the cetaceans (mammals) there are many types of dolphins and whales, to multitudes of tropical fish, manta ray, octopus, shark, and turtle. It's no wonder there's never a dull moment on the water.

The sky is home to many birds seen catching fish every day from the rocks or swooping across the ocean. The Indian Flying Fox (Fruit Bat) don't seem to know that they're reputation is for being a creature of the night. They dart across blue skies and turquoise lagoons to hang upside down from the trees.

The winds of euphoria
are lullibyes for
a soothing dream

it should come
as no surprise
it goes great
with ice cream!!

Journal Entry:

Creative visualization is a real thing.

When I was a child, I saw a cartoon where a man encounters a magic genie. The genie, as usual, grants the man one wish. The man asks for 100 bags of gold, which promptly falls from the sky, crushing him to death. I thought to myself then, "Okay. I must properly phrase my request so that I don't get tricked into death. My wish is to live past 100 but never to need assistance for basic personal care and hygiene, and to keep my memories." I concluded that if I make it to 100 years of age, with the accompanying requirements, in turn, it would mean everything along the way went okay.

There are unlimited fleeting desires to distract from what's important. When one distinctly understands their higher objectives, they can channel the energy of the universe to reach the goal.

For an artist, nearly every second of living is an opportunity for artistic expression. In this manner, we can strive to live in an eternal prolific state of mind and action.

To anyone who has ever built something or cooked a fantastic meal, they should understand the wonderful feeling of contentment derived from the creative process.

*An oasis of musical thoughts flows through my mind.
Each thought reverberates a different color note for note.*

From the deepest depths to the highest heights, the existence of math needn't be counted upon.

Rider Anko

my love for you
drives me forward
on an inexhaustible
path of auspiciousness

unconditionally, without
expectation, you inspire my very
motivations and aspirations

dreams to Reality

if patience is a virtue
then my resolve will
lead to purity

creative tenacity
in daily life

it's all predestined

i feel the future
deep within my being
as well as the past

the presence is
humble perseverance

we are children
of woman, man, and Earth

The Meaning of Life

Humans have perfected survival well enough to have tons of free time to ponder what it all means, and from where we came. The Maldives has attracted the world's most renowned scientists to ponder upon its creation. In 1842, Charles Darwin presented his theory after studying coral atolls in the Atlantic and Pacific Oceans.

Darwin said that the coral reef grew along the edges of volcanos that rose from the ocean. After a volcano receded, the reefs remained circular, protecting a lagoon within. Over time, these lagoons filled in with dead coral and organic materials. Thus the islands were born.

In more recent times, scientists discovered that fish have greatly assisted in the formation of the islands. Parrotfish eat coral polyps. The excrement of this stony coral has built entire fine-sand beaches.

Journal Entry:

As we compare ourselves to the changing demands of family, peers, and society at large, the human condition and norm are changing too. Relative to the universe and greater spirituality, these changes are minute. But, in our cerebral hemispheres, we are playing a constant game of catch up. By the time we think we've caught up, the tangible transitions form and meaning. It's a test of our ability to cope and accept our mission.

Us, who are catching the rhythm of these transformations, and not getting stuck at the junctions, are the ones who will be qualified leaders to the next generations. Our ability to roll with the punches, take leaps of faith, and follow our hearts through a labyrinth of metamorphoses will become the legends that set standards.

Rider: Farey

*I have to cruise
Let the wind go
through my mind
trying to find
something inside to
take me yet another
step beyond
what I see
and already
know*

Mystery Rider

from here beckons the ever-elusive object of my profound desire

Life is a story composition
and I, its designer

The "great mystery" conveys signs through
intuition and circumstance.

These signs are the
elements in hand to
design the story of my life.

A story can be told in fractions of a second.
Such is the consuming parameters
of time and mind.

It matters not how long a life is;
a minute, day, month, or century;
for time is a canvas,
memories the paint and even
a blank canvas tells a story.

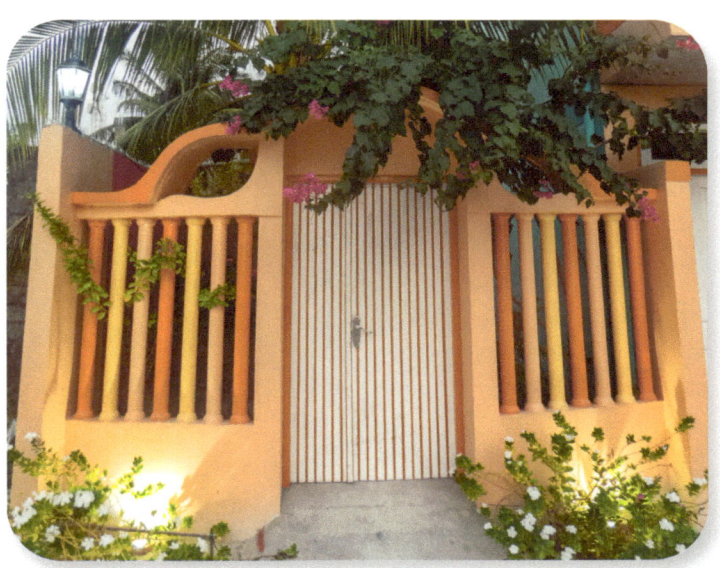

the meaning of life is to make life meaningful

The greatest rewards await those who truly learn how to move through life with command over their ego vs. the ego's control.

Epilogue: Ego

Speaking on the part of sports and athletes, surfers are easily susceptible to overbearing egocentricity. It's not a team sport and wholly revolves around the individual.

Arguably, the learning phases of surfing can be the most purely blissful moments. The intrigue upon initiation and falling in love with the magic of riding a wave is undeniable. As the person evolves into a surfer with ability, they often grow aware of their impression on others. The glory of surfing can feel quite glamorous.

Being conscious of watching eyes changes the experience and communion with the waves, ocean, and nature. With a bridled sense of ego, surfing is a more pure interaction with the environment. The emergence of our genuine self is imminent when we know we are alone. Our deeper intent becomes evident with no one to see our disappearance into the sea. Indeed, it's best to have a partner to practice the buddy system. Common knowledge says it's not smart to enter the ocean if there´s nobody else around. It's a quick way to shed layers of ego for a few minutes, at least. On the other hand, if you have loved ones expecting you to return home, endangering your safety by surfing solo could also be considered selfish.

Be humble.

Like breaking open a
coconut or watermelon,
destiny is busted
open to manifestation, and
we rejoice in the fruits of labor.

In this same way,
the rains brings about this
dynamic renewal and
thrival.

With the bolt of lightning and clap of thunder the clouds are burst open and my heart is drenched and cleansed in the nectar of transcendence and destiny.

My arrogance is struck down and my awareness raised, filled to the brim with lucid consciousness.

Rider Anko

The author surfing in the rain
Photo: Laurent Masurel

Author's Bio

Thirumoolar Devar, aka "Moolar" or simply, "Moo," was born in Manhattan, New York City. He grew up in a Tamil founded, yet multi-ethnic Kundalini yoga ashram. He learned about world religions and spirituality while traveling around the United States until age 15 when he became an independent. He worked in tourism and hospitality since early on, with a majority of U.S. years spent in New Orleans. There he became interested in the arts, playing music, and practicing photography since the young age of 7 in 1977.

After studying graphic design at California Institute of the Arts (CalArts), he began his career in the publishing industry at a small-town newspaper in Bay St. Louis, Mississippi. Right at the digital transition, he helped them make the switch from the old paste-up process to modern computer-based production.

Returning to school to study digital video at The American Film Institute (AFI) in Hollywood, he then continued west to Maui, Hawaii. There he began his freelance operations working for the tour and activity vendors throughout the Hawaiian islands. In the year 2000, he began learning web development. Shortly after that, he traveled to his first foreign land. By 2009 he was living abroad fulltime, filling his passport with stamps from around the globe. From a remote international office, he works online, making websites and books under the name Studio With A View.

Moolar makes the analogy of his paths traversed to the juxtaposition of The Force and The Darkside from the classic movie, Star Wars. However, his favorite film is Blade Runner. When he was a young boy, he enjoyed reading the adventurous tales of Tarzan and other Edgar Rice Burroughs books. Two Herman Hesse books that influenced him in his teens were Narcissus and Goldmund and Steppenwolf. His life's journey unfolded by diving headfirst and unabashedly into the exploration of both the internal and external pleasures and pains of existence.

In 2020 he launched his publishing company, Earth Afloat. The company's first self-published books are a series of short stories written by his father, "Fables Found - A Treasure of Wisdom for Grandchildren."

Moo continues to travel the globe and helps other authors and storytellers to publish their works, both fiction and non-fiction.

www.EarthAfloatPublishing.com
BLOG: www.EarthAfloat.com
PHOTO MAP: www.NomadicRefuge.com
FINE ART PHOTOGRAPHY: www.TheIntenseCalm.com
PRODUCTION & DESIGN SERVICES: www.StudioWithAView.com

www.FablesFound.com

BLOG: www.EarthAfloat.com

Photo Map: www.NomadicRefuge.com

Fine Art Photo: www.TheIntenseCalm.com

Fables Found
A Treasure of Wisdom for Grandchildren

By L. Devar

What is your favorite childhood fable? You may remember stories that concluded with an insightful moral based on life's common teachings such as, "slow and steady wins the race."

This book of fables follows in the age-old tradition of using fascinating animal behavior to illuminate the timeless lessons to our younger generations, so they themselves can grow to be wise grandparents.

In delightful style, each fable is preceded by a poem. The stage is then set in an alternate location; however, always founded on a conversation between a grandparent and grandchild.

We have been informed and formed by numerous symbolic myths and legends. They are wonderful tools for us to pass on the values, standards, and truths we consider essential in our lives and for the growth of our offspring.

In this traditional manner of parables handed down from cultures around the world, we tell of our observations and experience to plant ideas and principles worthy of cultivation.

May all creatures find happiness.

www.ingramcontent.com/pod-product-compliance
Lightning Source LLC
Chambersburg PA
CBHW042247100526
44587CB00002B/47